BIBLICAL RELIGION
AND
THE SEARCH
FOR ULTIMATE REALITY

BIBLICAL RELIGION
AND
THE SEARCH
FOR ULTIMATE REALITY

BY

PAUL TILLICH

THE UNIVERSITY OF CHICAGO PRESS

The James W. Richard Lectures
in the Christian Religion
University of Virginia
1951–52

THE UNIVERSITY OF CHICAGO PRESS, CHICAGO 60637
THE UNIVERSITY OF CHICAGO PRESS, LTD., LONDON

© *The University of Chicago 1955. Published 1955*
Ninth Impression 1972
Printed in the United States of America
International Standard Book Number: 0–226–80340–6 (clothbound)
Library of Congress Catalog Card Number: 55–5149

To John Dillenberger

This book is a slightly extended version of the James W. Richard Lectures which I delivered at the University of Virginia in the fall of 1951. The subject of the book is a central problem of systematic theology, and it is an especially urgent question of my own theological thought. The philosophical language I am using in my theological work has often been critically contrasted with the concrete imagery of the biblical language. The larger part of this book describes the contrast in its most radical form. But I do not draw the consequence, expressed by some of my critics, that theology has to restrain itself from using philosophical terms. It is my conviction that this is neither possible nor desirable and that the attempt to do it leads to self-deception or primitivism. In contrast to such attempts, I try to show that each of the biblical symbols drives inescapably to an ontological question and that the answers given by theology necessarily contain ontological elements. A development of the answers, of course, would have been beyond the scope of these lectures; a full development can be done only within a theological system. This is the reason for the relative brevity of the last chapters.

I want to express my thanks to the University of Virginia and to the Richard Lecture Foundation for the invitation to give the lectures; to the University of Chicago Press, which made this publication possible; and to my friend and colleague John Dillenberger (to whom the book is dedicated), who has—as so often in the past—revised the text of my manuscript in a most helpful way.

NEW YORK CITY
June 1955

TABLE OF CONTENTS

ix

BASIC CONCEPTS

1. *The Meaning of "Biblical Religion"*

The title "Biblical Religion and the Search for Ultimate Reality" itself may have raised a number of skeptical questions. This skepticism may be increased when I say that, in spite of the tremendous tension between biblical religion and ontology, they have an ultimate unity and a profound interdependence. In reaction to such a statement some will certainly ask: Is not the very nature of biblical religion opposed to philosophy? Does not biblical religion destroy the strongholds of human thought by the power of the divine revelation to which it gives witness? Was not the great theological event of the last decades Karl Barth's prophetic protest against the synthesis between Christianity and humanism? Did not Barth reinterpret for our time the radical dissociation of Christianity and philosophy found in Kierkegaard a century ago? Is not the conviction that the advancement and the application of the gospel are served in the attempt to relate philosophy and biblical religion an unfortunate return to the theological situation at the turn of the century? These are among the questions which will concern us throughout this analysis.

The term "biblical religion" poses some problems. If the Bible is considered to be the document of God's final self-manifestation, in what sense can one speak of biblical religion? Religion is a function of the human mind; according to recent theologians, it is the futile attempt of man to reach God. Religion moves from man toward God, while revelation moves from God to man, and its first work is to confound man's religious aspirations. There are many students of theology, especially in Continental Europe, who contrast divine revelation not only with philosophy but also with religion. For them religion and philosophy stand under the same condemnation, since both are attempts of man to be like God; both are demonic elevations of man above his creatureliness and finitude. And, of the two, religion is the more dangerous, because philosophy, at least in principle, can be restricted to the technical problems of logic and epistemology. If this were true, a confrontation of philosophy and biblical religion would be impossible, because there would not be such a thing as biblical religion. And philosophy would be either harmless logical inquiry or demonic *hubris*. The adjective "biblical" would demand "revelation" and not "religion" as its noun.

We must take this argument seriously. It may be surprising to Americans to know that I have been strongly criticized by German readers of my books because the word "religion" appears frequently in them. Although these critics are in sympathy with my general point of view, they cannot understand that a modern theologian would use the word "religion" in a positive sense. For them, the greater part of what we call "religion" is the devil's work. To *Criticism* speak of "biblical religion" is to deprive the Bible of its revelatory character and to consider it a work of men or, even worse, a demonic creation.

But, in saying this, these people show that they too have a religion. They forget that revelation must be received and that the name for the reception of revelation is "religion." They forget that revelation becomes more revealing the more it speaks to man in his concrete situation, to the special receptivity of his mind, to the special conditions of his society, and to the special historical period. Revelation is never revelation in general, however universal its claim may be. It is always revelation for someone and for a group in a definite environment, under unique circumstances. Therefore, he who receives revelation witnesses to it in terms of his individuality and in terms of the social and spiritual conditions in which the revelation has been manifested to him. In other words, he does it in terms of his religion. This makes the concept "biblical religion" meaningful. Every passage of the Old and New Testaments is both revelation and religion. The Bible is a document both of the divine self-manifestation and of the way in which human beings have received it. And it is not that some words and sentences belong to the former and others to the latter but that in one and the same passage revelation and the reception of revelation are inseparably united. He who gives an account of divine revelation simultaneously gives an account of his own religion. The basic error of fundamentalism is that it overlooks the contribution of the receptive side in the revelatory situation and consequently identifies *one* individual and conditioned form of receiving the divine with the divine itself. But there are other forms. Even in the Bible we find differences between the priestly and the prophetic writings, between early and late traditions in the Four Gospels. We find them, too, in the classics of church history and in the denominational interpretations of the Bible today. These different ways characterize the religious side of the biblical and church tradition; they are receptacles of revelation.

own
situation
etc.

4

Revelation cannot be separated from them. Those who ignore this situation are forced to deny the differences on the receptive side and to confuse their own form of reception with an assumedly undiluted and untransformed revelation. But there is no pure revelation. Wherever the divine is manifest, it is manifest in "flesh," that is, in a concrete, physical, and historical reality, as in the religious receptivity of the biblical writers. This is what biblical religion means. It is itself a highly dialectical concept.

2. The Meaning of Philosophy

This character of biblical literature makes possible and necessary the confrontation of biblical religion with philosophy. But a confrontation would be impossible if philosophy were logical analysis and epistemological inquiry only, however important may be the development of these tools for philosophical thought. Yet philosophy, "love of wisdom," means much more than this. It seems to me that the oldest definition given to philosophy is, at the same time, the newest and that which always was and always will be valid: Philosophy is that cognitive endeavor in which the question of being is asked. In accordance with this definition, Aristotle summarized the development of Greek philosophy, anticipating the consequent periods up to the Renaissance and preparing the modern ways of asking the same question. The question of being is not the question of any special being, its existence and nature, but it is the question of what it means to *be*. It is the simplest, most profound, and absolutely inexhaustible question—the question of what it means to say that something *is*. This word "is" hides the riddle of all riddles, the mystery that there is anything at all. Every philosophy, whether it asks the question of being openly or not, moves around this mystery, has a partial answer to it, whether acknowledged or not, but is generally at a loss to answer it fully. Philosophy is always in what the Greeks called *aporia* ("without a way"), that is, in a state of perplexity about the nature of being. For this inquiry I like to use the word "ontology," derived from *logos* ("the word") and *on* ("being"); that is, the word of being, the word which grasps being, makes its nature manifest, drives it out of its hiddenness into the light of knowledge. Ontology is the center of all philosophy. It is, as Aristotle has called it, "first philosophy," or, as it was unfortunately also called, "metaphysics," that which follows the physical books in the collection of Aristotelian writings. This name was and is unfortunate, because it conveys the misconception that ontology deals with transempirical realities, with a world behind the world, existing only in speculative imagination. In all areas of theology—historical, practical, systematic—there are theologians who believe that they can avoid the confrontation of philosophy and biblical religion by identifying philosophy with what they call "metaphysical speculation," which they can then throw onto the garbage heap of past errors, intellectual and moral. I want to challenge as strongly as possible all those who use this language to tell us what they mean by metaphysics and speculation and, after they have done so, to compare their description with what the classical philosophers from Anaximander to Whitehead have done. *Speculari,* the root of the word "speculation," means "looking at something." It has nothing to do with the creation of imaginary worlds, an accusation which the philosophers could make against the theologians with equal justification. It is infuriating to see how biblical theologians, when explaining the concepts of the Old or New Testament writers, use most of the terms created by the toil of philosophers and the ingenuity of the speculative mind and then dismiss, with cheap denunciations, the work from which their language has been immensely enriched. No theologian should be taken seriously as a theologian, even if he is a great Christian and a great scholar, if his work shows that he does not take philosophy seriously.

Therefore, to avoid the "black magic" of words like "metaphysical speculation," let us speak of ontology as the basic work of those who aspire to wisdom (*sophia* in Greek, *sapientia* in Latin), meaning the knowledge of the principles. And, more specifically, let us speak of ontological *analysis* in order to show that one has to look at things as they are given if one wants to discover the principles, the structures, and the nature of being as it is embodied in everything that is.

On the basis of such an ontological analysis, philosophy tries to show the presence of being and its structures in the different realms of being, in nature and in man, in history and in value, in knowledge and in religion. But in each case it is not the subject matter as such with which philosophy deals but the constitutive principles of being, that which is always present if a thing participates in the power to be and to resist nonbeing.

Philosophy in this sense is not a matter of liking or disliking. It is a matter of man as man, for man is that being who asks the question of being. Therefore, every human being philosophizes, just as every human being moralizes and acts politically, artistically, scientifically, religiously. There are immense differences in degree, education, and creativity among different human beings in the exercise of these functions, but there is no difference in the character of the function itself. The child's restless question, "Why is this so; why is that not so?" and Kant's grandiose description, in his critique of the cosmological argument, of the God who asks himself, "Why am I?" are the same in substance although infinitely distinguished in form. Man is by nature a philosopher, because he inescapably asks the question of being. He does it in myth and epic, in drama and poetry, in the structure and the vocabulary of any language.

It is the special task of philosophy to make this question conscious and to elaborate the answers methodologically. The prephilosophical ways of putting and answering the question of being prepare the philosophical way. When philosophy comes into its own, it is not without a long prehistory. Without Homer's poetry, the Dionysian festivals, and the Solonic laws, and, above all, without the genius of the Greek language, no Western philosophy as we have it now would have developed. And everyone who participates in the language and the art and the cult and the social life of a culture is a collaborator in the creation of its philosophy. He is a prephilosophical philosopher, and most people are in this situation even after a methodical philosophy has been born. But one thing has changed since this birth: not only does prephilosophy determine philosophy but also philosophy determines prephilosophy. The language in nonphilosophical literature and common usage, which is a form of prephilosophy too, is determined by previous philosophical usage. Nor do those who are antiphilosophical escape this. Even the despiser of philosophy is not only a collaborator with, but also a pupil of, the subject of his contempt. This interdependence between prephilosophy and philosophy is also true of the biblical and all other religious and theological literature, even if written under a strong, antiphilosophical bias. The fundamentalist minister who said to me, "Why do we need philosophy when we possess all truth through revelation?" did not realize that, in using the words "truth" and "revelation," he was determined by a long history of philosophical thought which gave these words the meaning in which he used them. We cannot avoid philosophy, because the ways we take to avoid it are carved out and paved by philosophy.

HUMAN EXISTENCE AND THE QUESTION OF BEING

1. *Man and the Question of Being*

One can rightly say that man is the being who is able to ask questions. Let us think for a moment what it means to ask a question. It implies, first, that we do not have that for which we ask. If we had it, we would not ask for it. But, in order to be able to ask for something, we must have it partially; otherwise it could not be the object of a question. He who asks has and has not at the same time. If man is that being who asks the question of being, he has and has not the being for which he asks. He is separated from it while belonging to it. Certainly we belong to being—its power is in us—otherwise we would not be. But we are also separated from it; we do not possess it fully. Our power of being is limited. We are a mixture of being and nonbeing. This is precisely what is meant when we say that we are finite. It is man in his finitude who asks the question of being. He who is infinite does not ask the question of being, for, as infinite, he has the complete power of being. He is identical with it; he is God. And a being which does not realize that it is finite (and in our actual experience that is every being except man) cannot ask, because it cannot go beyond itself and its limits. But man can and must ask; he cannot avoid asking, because he belongs to the power of being from which he is separated, and he knows both that he belongs to it and that he is separated from it.

We have called our subject "biblical religion and the search for ultimate reality." This gives an excellent interpretation of what is meant by being in the sense of the ontological question. The word "ultimate" here points to a reality which is only preliminary. Both words, "ultimate" and "preliminary," are temporal metaphors, but they express the way in which we encounter our world. Everything we encounter appears to us as real, as true being. But we soon notice that its reality is only transitory. It was, but now it is no more. Nonbeing has swallowed it, so to speak. Or we notice that it is different from what it seemed to be, and we distinguish between its surface and its deeper, more real levels. But soon these levels also prove to be surface, and we try to penetrate into still deeper levels, toward the ultimate reality of a thing. No thing, however, is isolated from all other things. And, the deeper the levels into which we enter, the less possible it is to consider them in separation from each other and from the whole of reality. In the ordinary encounter of man with man, each appears as an isolated individual. Yet, if we enter the levels of personal existence which have been rediscovered by depth psychology, we encounter the past, the ancestors, the collective unconscious, the living substance in which all living beings participate. In our search for the "really real" we are driven from one level to another to a point where we cannot speak of level any more, where we must ask for that which is the ground of all levels, giving them their structure and their power of being. The search for ultimate reality beyond everything that seems to be real is the search for being-itself, for the power of being in everything that is. It is the ontological question, the root question of every philosophy.

The preceding considerations enlarge our understanding of the human situation. We philosophize because we are finite and because we know that we are finite. We are a mixture of being and nonbeing, and we are aware of it. We have seen that we encounter a world to which we belong and which, in our encounter with it, shows the same mixture of being and nonbeing as does our human predicament. Therefore, we must say: It is our finitude in interdependence with the finitude of our world which drives us to search for ultimate reality. This search is a consequence of our encounter as finite beings with a finite world. Because we stand between being and nonbeing and long for a form of being that prevails against nonbeing in ourselves and in our world, we philosophize. If this is a true description of the human situation, there can be no doubt that the philosophical question is as genuine and inescapable as the religious question and that the confrontation of ontology and biblical religion is a necessary task.

2. Philosophical Objections

Before turning to those characteristics of biblical religion which are relevant for such a confrontation, we must deal with possible objections to our understanding of the nature of philosophy. Everybody will agree that only philosophy can decide what philosophy shall be, since there is no cognitive sphere above it which could make the decision. Yet it is neither fair to other philosophies nor adequate to the confrontation of philosophy and biblical religion if only *one* understanding of philosophy is brought to such a confrontation. But the crucial question is whether the definition of the ontological question is the mark of only one type of philosophy or whether it is something universally human and in its methodological elaboration something universally philosophical? Before answering this question, we must settle two problems. The first is the question of whether it is meaningful to define a term which has a very long and rich history in a way which completely contradicts this history. Some representatives of modern logic, while rejecting the whole of philosophy before the rise of logical positivism and semantic analysis, nevertheless are willing to use the term "philosophy" for their own endeavors. For them the ontological question is meaningless and without cognitive value. It belongs to the realm of emotion and can, at best, lead to an aesthetic expression of feelings. If they are right, the confrontation of what *they* call philosophy with biblical religion would be as absurd as the confrontation of electrophysics and biblical religion. However, some of their representatives have become aware of the limitations of their work and have admitted that there are significant statements outside the realm of pure and applied logical calculus. Some of them might even admit that an ontological statement could be significant. And they should admit it, for their own statements about the relation of knowledge and reality are significant ontological assertions, even if they are not true. And, if ontological statements are considered at all significant, their relation to religious expression is a genuine problem.

② The second problem is raised by ontologists themselves. They question the term "being" from the standpoint of the philosophy of process. Being seems to point to a static world, a block reality, whereas reality irrefutably has the character of becoming. One must agree that a definition of ontology which gives preference to the static over the dynamic elements in reality not only is prejudiced and mistaken but also has serious consequences for the confrontation of philosophy and biblical religion. A static ultimate and the living God are obviously incompatible. But being-as-such has neither static nor dynamic implications. It precedes any special qualification. It points to the original fact that there is something and not nothing and to the power of that which is to resist nonbeing. Obviously, this resistance has a dynamic character, and the power of being is actual in many centers of power. But they all participate in the power of being, in being-itself.

This also answers a third objection, coming from
③ an empiricist philosophy. Here the ontological ques-

tion is not denied, but it is interpreted as the question of the most general structures and relations of reality and the methods of their analysis. Concepts like being-itself or the power of being seem to be idealistic or mystical—in any case, beyond empirical confirmation. Here it is my aim to show that the ontological question underlies even this type of philosophy. As in the two previous arguments, this is the case. In terms of the history of philosophy, it is a nominalistic ontology which has determined philosophical empiricism from the high Middle Ages to the present moment. Being, according to this vision of reality, is characterized by individualization and not by participation. All individual things, including men and their minds, stand alongside each other, looking at each other and at the whole of reality, trying to penetrate step by step from the periphery toward the center, but having no immediate approach to it, no direct participation in other individuals and in the universal power of being which makes for individualization. The immense historical significance of this philosophy as well as the limits of its view of reality cannot be discussed here. But one thing must be emphasized. It is a view of reality as a whole. It assumes a structure of being, though different from other possible assumptions of being, as that of medieval realism, which today is called "idealism." It is an ontology of a special type, but it does not change the basic understanding of philosophy. Even if it resists ontology, it presupposes an answer to the ontological question—the question of being.

3. The Philosophical Attitude

A last consideration may conclude this discussion of the meaning of philosophy. It is the question of the philosophical attitude. A description of the way in which the ontological problem arises out of the human situation universally implies that in every genuine philosophy two functions of the human mind are effective. One of them is usually called "theoretical"; the other, "existential." The philosopher faces reality with that astonishment which is the beginning of all knowledge. He makes discoveries, states them, and rejects them on the basis of new discoveries. He enters into conversations with others who are grasped by the same desire for knowledge. Through "Yes" and "No," errors are overcome and reality discloses itself to the mind. Successful research leads to the establishment of methods and criteria which can be used for many objects of inquiry. Ways of verification are sought and found. Some all-pervading principles are discovered and distinguished from the continuous flux of things and events. For thousands of years every philosopher has tried to define these principles, usually called "categories," and their relation to mind and reality. And, finally, he transcends even them and tries to reach being-itself, the ultimate aim of thought. He does this, not in order to define it—which is impossible, since it is the presupposition of every definition—but to point to that which is always present and always escaping. All this is done with the same strictness, the same logical and methodological rationality, with which a mathematician or a physicist or a historian works. But the philosopher is driven from one step to another and to the last step, the question of being-itself, by something else, the existential element. This "something else" can be called with Plato the *eros* for the idea, or with the Stoics the desire for wisdom, or with Augustine the longing for the truth-itself, or with Spinoza the intellectual love of the substance, or with Hegel the passion for the absolute, or with Hume the liberation from prejudice, or with Nietzsche the will to participate in the creative and destructive life-processes. It is always a driving force in the depths of his being that makes the philosopher a philosopher. The question of ultimate reality is produced not by a theoretical interest in abstraction from the totality of man's being but by this rare union of passion and rationality. This combination makes the philosopher great. His existence is involved in his question; therefore, he asks the question of ultimate reality—the question of being-itself. On the other hand, the existential element does not swallow the theoretical. In contrast to the saint, prophet, and poet, the philosopher's passion for the infinite pours into his cognitive function. He wants to *know;* he wants to know what being means, what its structures are, and how one can penetrate into its mystery. He is a philosopher.

· III ·

THE FOUNDATION OF BIBLICAL PERSONALISM

1. The Personal Character of the Experience of the Holy

In the first chapter we attempted an elucidation of the two basic concepts, ontology and biblical religion, and discussed the nature and the necessity of the search for ultimate reality. We now turn to an analysis of the character of biblical religion and to the questions raised by its confrontation with ontology. In doing so, we are aware of what has been discussed in the first chapter—that the term "biblical religion" stands for two things: divine revelation and human reception.

As human reception, biblical religion belongs to the whole of the history of religion. Everyone who knows something about the historical settings of biblical religion knows how much they were influenced by the surrounding religions and how many analogies can be drawn between biblical and other religions. But this does not affect the Christian judgment that in the biblical forms of human reception which belong to the history of religion revelation is present, not merely as one revelation among others, but as the criterion of all other revelations, past and future.

It is my intention to present some traits of biblical religion (and implicitly of revelation) in their radical and uncompromising character. They will not be watered down to the point where it is easy to unite them with the search for ultimate reality. In fact, I want to give a picture of those traits of biblical religion which inescapably drive toward a conflict with ontology. The center of the antiontological bias of biblical religion is its personalism. According to every word of the Bible, God reveals himself as personal. The encounter with him and the concepts describing this encounter are thoroughly personal. How can these concepts be brought into a synthesis with the search for ultimate reality? This is the central question.

There is no type of religion which does not personify the holy which is encountered by man in his religious experience. In every religion the experience of the holy is mediated by some piece of finite reality. Everything can become a medium of revelation, a bearer of divine power. "Everything" not only includes all things in nature and culture, in soul and history; it also includes principles, categories, essences, and values. Through stars and stones, trees and animals, growth and catastrophe; through tools and houses, sculpture and melody, poems and prose, laws and customs; through parts of the body and functions of the mind, family relations and voluntary communities, historical leaders and national elevation; through time and space, being and nonbeing, ideals and virtues, the holy can encounter us. Everything that is, really or ideally, has become a medium of the divine mystery sometime in the course of the history of religion. But, in the moment in which something took on this role, it also received a personal face. Even tools and stones and categories became personal in the religious encounter, the encounter with the holy. *Persona,* like the Greek *prosopon,* points to the individual and at the same time universally meaningful character of the actor on the stage. For person is more than individuality. "Person" is individuality on the human level, with self-relatedness and world-relatedness and therefore with rationality, freedom, and responsibility. It is established in the encounter of an ego-self with another self, often called the "I-thou" relationship, and it exists only in community with other persons. These basic characteristics of personal being include others, such as the possibility of asking and receiving answers, as previously described. When we speak of "personification" in the religious experience, we attribute all these characteristics to the bearers of the holy, although they do not actually have them. Neither a stone nor a virtue is self-related and has freedom and responsibility. In what sense, then, can we attribute personal qualities to a-personal beings? We can do this if we consider them not objects of a cognitive approach but elements of an encounter, namely, the encounter with the holy. They are parts of this encounter, not as things or values, but as bearers of something beyond themselves. This something beyond themselves is the holy, the numinous presence of that which concerns us ultimately. Man can experience the holy in and through everything, but, as the holy, it cannot be less than he is; it cannot be a-personal. Nothing that is less than we, nothing that encounters less than the center of our personality, can be of ultimate concern for us. It is meaningless to ask whether the holy *is* personal or whether its bearers *are* personal. If "is" and "are" express an objective, cognitive assertion, they certainly are *not* personal. But this is not the question. The question is what becomes of them as elements of the religious encounter? And then the answer is clearly that they become personal. Perhaps one should not speak of "personification," literally "making personal," because this seems to imply the fabrication of something untrue and artificial as a necessary concession to the primitive mind. The personal encounter in religious experience is as real as the encounter of subject and object in the cognitive experience or the encounter of vision and meaning in the artistic experience. In this sense religious personalism expresses reality, namely, reality within the religious encounter.

Wherever the holy is experienced, the person-to-person character of this experience is obvious. It is easy to show that this is the case in the so-called 'primitive religions" and their personal divinities, however subhuman they may be. One deals with them as one deals with persons. It is equally easy to show the personal character of the encounter with the holy in the great mythological religions. All the gods of the myths are personal; they all are "thou's" for a human ego. Man can pray to them and influence them by sacrifice or moral behavior. Mysticism tries to transcend the ego-thou relation between God and man and does so successfully in the great mystics, at least in ecstatic moments. But the religions out of which mysticism has arisen, in India, China, Persia, and Europe, are personalistic. They have personal gods who are adored, even if one knows that beyond them there is the transpersonal *One*, the ground and abyss of everything personal. An Indian Brahman with whom I had a conversation about this point made it very clear to me that he stood in the transpersonalistic thinking of India's classical tradition but that, as a religious Hindu, he would say that the Brahman power makes itself personal for us. He did not attribute the personal element in religion only to man's subjectivity. He did not call it illusion; he described it as an inner quality of the transpersonal Brahman power. In every religion the holy is encountered in personal images.

2. The Special Character of Biblical Personalism

The personalism of biblical religion must be seen against the background of universal religion, representing it and, at the same time, denying it in a unique way. In the I-thou structure of the religious encounter the personalism of the Bible is like the personalism of any other religion. But it is different from the personalism of any other religion in its creation of an idea of personal relationship which is exclusive and complete. Every religion calls its God "thou," for instance, in a prayer. Biblical religion does the same, but it excludes elements from the

26

prayer which would transform it into a person-thing relation; for instance, the "do-ut-des" or bargain relationship which makes of the divine "thou" a means for one's ends. In fighting against such an attitude, biblical religion has discovered the full meaning of the personal. It is the unconditional character of the biblical God that makes the relation to him radically personal. For only that which concerns us in the center of our personal existence concerns us unconditionally. The God who is unconditional in power, demand, and promise is the God who makes us completely personal and who, consequently, is completely personal in our encounter with him. It is not that we first know what person is and then apply the concept of God to this. But, in the encounter with God, we first experience what person should mean and how it is distinguished from, and must be protected from, everything a-personal.

If biblical religion is not only personal but the source of the full meaning of *person*, how can the a-personal concept "being" be of ultimate concern and a matter of infinite passion? Is this first confrontation not also the last, namely, the end of all attempts to achieve a synthesis between ontology and biblical religion? Is not God in the religious encounter *a* person among others, related to them as an *I* to a *thou*, and vice versa? And, if so, is he not *a* being, while the ontological question asks the question of being-itself, of the power of being in and above all beings? In the ontological question, is not God himself transcended?

For the present we shall leave the question in this radical form and turn to some special expression of the personalism of biblical religion.

IV

PERSONALISM AND THE DIVINE-HUMAN RELATIONSHIP

1. The Reciprocal Character of the Divine-Human Relationship

Every relation between persons is based on free reciprocity. If one of the two in a relationship is not able to act *as* a person, an ego-thing relation replaces the ego-thou correlation. Although, in biblical religion, God is the one who gives and man the one who receives, reciprocity is always present in the divine-human relationship and expressed without any fear that it might limit the absolute divine supremacy. God reacts differently to different human actions. Logically, this means that he is partly dependent upon them. He would have reacted differently if man had acted in another way than he did act. This cannot be otherwise, because in a person-to-person relationship a personal action of the one side provokes a personal reaction on the other side. A reaction is personal if it originates in the free, responsible, and deciding center of the person. In the realm of a-personal objects, every reaction is determined by the action producing it, by the nature of the object acted upon, and by the universal context within which the action occurs. This is also partly so in the personal realm. But one new factor is added: the object acted upon is not fully determined because it is essentially subject. It is free to decide what it shall do; it is personal. Therefore, its reaction is only partly calculable and ultimately undetermined. This creates the living reciprocity of a person-to-person relationship. We act or speak, but we never know with certainty beforehand how we will react to the action of the other one. Every moment of a living relationship is characterized by an element of indeterminacy. This free reciprocity between God and man is the root of the dynamic character of biblical religion. God commands; man obeys or disobeys. God plans; man co-operates or contradicts. God promises; man believes or disbelieves. God threatens; man reacts with fear or arrogance or change of heart. And God's attitude changes accordingly. The threatening, wrathful God becomes a loving, merciful God. The judging and condemning God becomes a forgiving, saving God. Man prays, and God hears or does not hear. Man tries hard, and God rejects. Man waits, and God accepts. Man hates, and God answers with love. It is a free, personal reciprocity, subject to no pre-established rule. It is real life with all the unexpected, irrational, intimate qualities of a living relationship.

Nothing seems to contradict the ontological concept of "being" more than this reciprocity between God and man. How can a being act upon being-itself, how can being-itself be mutually related to any particular being? How can a being influence the ground of being in which and out of which it lives? How can being-itself change if, by definition, it transcends the categories of change, such as time, space, causality, and substance? Is not the God of free reciprocity subject to the categories which being-itself must transcend? Does not ontology dissolve all the relations of free reciprocity in which the biblical God stands? Is it not the deathblow for living religion and, above all, for biblical religion?

2. Biblical Personalism and the Word

A person-to-person relationship is actual through the word. One is related to a person in speaking to him, and one remains in relation to him only if he answers. Under certain conditions, signs and gestures can be substituted for the spoken word. But they have meaning only in reference to words, to the spoken language. Biblical personalism is most conspicuously manifest in the significance of the word in biblical literature. The Word of God, the words of the prophets, the words of Jesus, and the words of the apostles and preachers appear on every page of the Bible. Theological biblicism usually takes the form of a "theology of the word." It took this form in the Reformation, and it does so in the neo-Reformation theology of today. In the light of biblical personalism this is easy to understand. The word is directed to that in man which makes him a person, his rational, responsible, deciding center. The word mediates meaning which must be understood, judged, accepted, or rejected in a free interpretation and a free decision. All this is performed by man as a person. The word is addressed to the personal center. Revelation through the word respects man's freedom and his personal self-relatedness. Man is asked to listen, but he is left free to decline. He is not supposed to be overpowered by the word, as in sorcery, where the word is used as a physical cause, or in magic, where the word is used as a psychic cause, or in suggestive talk, where the word is used as an emotional cause. These uses of the word are possible, but they eliminate the essence of the word, its quality as the bearer of meaning. They appear in the Bible as in the whole history of religion, but they are opposed, reduced in importance, and almost annihilated in the biblical religion. The word as the bearer of meaning has an impact on all sides of man's spiritual life, on the whole personality. It is addressed to the intellect; it informs man about his situation, his actual and ideal relation to God, the world, and himself. It is addressed to the will, and this is foremost in the Old Testament and decisive in the New. The Word of God is, above all, the command of God, the expression of his will and purpose, the means of creating and ordering the universe, of legislating and directing nations and individuals, of ruling and fulfilling history as a whole. And the word is addressed to the heart of man in threat and promise, in wrath and love, in rejection and acceptance. The word speaks to the person as a whole, to the free, responsible, and deciding center of the person.

Ontology thinks in other categories. Being-itself is present in everything that is, and everything that is participates in being. We speak *to* somebody, but we participate *in* something. Ontological participation gives immediate awareness of something of which we are a part or which is a part of us. Listening to the spoken word gives mediated knowledge of the hidden thought and will of a person from whose centered self we are excluded. Whereas revelation through the word keeps him who reveals himself apart from him who receives revelation, ontology tries to penetrate into the power of being which we encounter when we meet ourselves. Subject and object, in ontological research, are, so to speak, at one and the same place. They do not speak to each other. It seems as though ontology takes the word away from the God of revelation and makes him silent. Here again we leave the question in its most radical form and turn to other elements of biblical religion.

V

PERSONALISM AND THE DIVINE MANIFESTATIONS

1. *Personalism and Creation*

According to biblical religion, all divine manifestations are manifestations through the word. This refers first of all to creation. Biblical personalism is most obviously distinguished from the personalism of other religions by the doctrine of creation. This doctrine was the point at which the early church fought a life-and-death struggle against the religious movements of the later ancient world. It was the point at which the church held to the Old Testament as its own presupposition. The doctrine of creation is the one on which the doctrines of the Christ, of salvation and fulfilment, depend. Without it, Christianity would have ceased to exist as an independent movement. The doctrine of creation has two main functions. First, it emphasizes the dependence on God of everything created and, consequently, the essential goodness of creation. It protects the Christian interpretation of existence against a dualistic split between a good and an evil god. It preserves the personal unity of the one God. Second, it emphasizes the infinite distance between the Creator and the creature. It places the created outside the creative ground. It denies any participation of the creature in the creative substance out of which it comes. It is the doctrine of creation through the word which makes especially sharp the distance between the Creator and creation. It was correct and proper when later Jewish and Christian theologians spoke of creation out of nothing. This is an implication of creation through the word. It means that there is no substance, divine or antidivine, out of which finite beings receive their being. They receive it through the word, the will of God and its creative expression. The doctrine of creation through the word denies any substantial participation of man in God. It replaces substantial identity by personal distance.

Ontology speaks of being-itself as the ground of everything that is. It speaks of the one substance out of which all finite beings are made. It speaks of the identity of the infinite with the finite. It speaks of the finite mind through which the Absolute Mind wills and recognizes himself. It seems as though ontology dissolves the infinite into the finite or the finite into the infinite. Ontology seems to deprive God of his creative Word. It falls either into metaphysical dualism or into metaphysical monism. In both cases it removes the distance between God and man which is so powerfully expressed in biblical religion.

2. Personalism and Christology

Biblical personalism comes to its fulfilment in the message that the divine Word was incarnate in a personal life, in the life of Jesus, who for this reason is called the Christ. Biblical religion in the Old and New Testaments is a religion of personalities who, in the power of the Spirit of God, mediate the will of God and preserve the covenant between God and Israel, between God and mankind. The God who is encountered as a person acts in history through persons and their inner experiences. Indeed, there are many nonpersonal elements in the religion of the Old as well as the New Testament: communal traditions, ritual laws, legal orders, sacramental activities, scriptures, and hierarchies. Without these religious objectifications biblical religion could not have lived, survived, and produced an uninterrupted series of personalities. On the other hand, these objectifications are dependent on and transformed by the great personalities. Their experiences and struggles

37

and messages created the spirit of biblical religion. But in all of them the revelation mediated through them can still be separated from their persons. It is the revealing word, received by prophet or apostle, which makes him the medium of the divine self-manifestation, though he could not have received it without a personal life, open to the divine Word. But it is not this personal life as such which is revelatory; it is not his being but something mediated through his being. Jesus also used the prophetic words. But, beyond this, his words are expressions of his being, and they are this in unity with his deeds and sufferings. Together, they all point to a personal center which is completely determined by the divine presence, by the "Spirit without limit." This makes him Jesus the Christ. The Word appears *as* a person and only secondarily in the words of a person. The Word, the principle of the divine self-manifestation, appearing as a person, is the fulfilment of biblical personalism. It means that God is so personal that we see what he is only in a personal life. God can become man, because man is person and because God is personal. And, on the other hand, when God appears in a person, it becomes manifest what person should be. The limits of man's personal existence are overcome; the a-personal elements which try to enter and to disrupt personal existence are removed. The personal center rules the whole man because it is united with the personal center of the divine life.

The ontological question, the question of being, in and beyond everything that is, seems to depersonalize reality. The Logos, who for biblical religion can reveal the heart of divinity only in a concrete personal life, is, for ontology, present in everything. Ontology generalizes, while biblical religion individualizes. The search for ultimate reality seems to by-pass that concrete reality in which the ultimate is personally present. The universal Logos seems to draw into itself and to swallow the Logos who became flesh, that is, historical reality, in the personal life of an individual self. And the question arises: Is there any possibility of uniting ontology with biblical religion, if ontology could not accept the central assertion of biblical religion that Jesus is the Christ?

3. Personalism, History, and Eschatology

Biblical religion has a historical view of reality. The stories of the Old Testament are not only legends of the past history of Israel. This they are, too; but, beyond this, they are reports about the deeds of God who *works* for his ultimate aim, the establishment of his rule over Israel and over all mankind. The ideas of the covenant between Yahweh and his people, the ideas of the remnant and the messianic age, the message of Jesus that the rule of the heavens is at hand, the feeling of the early Christians of standing between two eras (i.e., between fulfilled and unfulfilled eschatology)—all this is a historical interpretation of history. And not only of history, for the whole universe is seen in historical perspective. The covenant symbol is applied not only to the relation between God and the nation but also to the relation between God and nature. The orders of nature are analogous to the order of the moral law. Nature cannot break them, and God will not break them. Man alone can break and has broken the covenant with God. But even then God will not break it; he will carry it through in history. Cosmic beginning and cosmic end are in this way drawn into the historical vision of reality. They are not cosmological necessities in the sense in which the Stoics speak of the burning of the world at the beginning and the end of every period. They are prehistorical but not unhistorical conditions of history. The historical vision of biblical religion makes even the universe historical.

In this cosmic frame the history of salvation occurs. History is the history of salvation in biblical religion. From the prehistorical fall of Adam to the posthistorical reunion of everything in God there is one straight line, starting with Noah and Abraham and ending with the second coming of the Christ. History is neither the expression of man's natural potentialities nor the tragic circle of man's growth and decay; history creates the new. In Christ a new Being has appeared within the world process; history has received a meaning and a center.

Corresponding to the transhistorical-historical beginning of the world process, biblical religion expects its historical-transhistorical end. Biblical religion is eschatological. It thinks in terms of a complete transformation of the structure of the new earth, the renewal of the whole of reality. And this new reality is the goal toward which history runs, and with it the whole universe, in a unique, irreversible movement.

Again we ask: How can this be united with the search for ultimate reality? Is not ontology the attempt to analyze the immovable structures of reality? And is not the concept of being-itself, in which everything that is participates, necessarily unhistorical? Does not the ontological interpretation of reality inescapably exclude the historically new? Does it not, particularly, interpret human sin and divine grace as ontological necessities, thus depriving sin of its character as a free, responsible act of man's personal center, and grace of its character as the free, personal act of the divine mercy? Are sin and grace, if taken into an ontological frame of reference, still sin and grace? And, further, if the new in history is excluded, can one speak of a purpose of the world process? Can one maintain the eschatological world view, the transcendent origin and the transcendent end of everything that is? Does not ontology undercut the meaning of hope in biblical religion?

We have discussed biblical personalism in some of its main doctrinal expressions, but we have omitted one whole side of biblical religion: its understanding of man and his situation. This will be the first task of the next chapter. Yet, if we look at the results of this chapter, it seems that no further chapter is possible. The confrontations of biblical religion and its personalism with the impersonalism of ontology seem to rule out any attempt at a synthesis. It will be the task of a part of the following chapter and of the last to show that this is not so and that each side needs the other for its own realization. But this relation is by no means to be found on the surface. It is necessary to penetrate deeply into both the nature of biblical religion and the nature of ontology in order to discover their profound interdependence.

· VI ·

MAN IN THE LIGHT OF BIBLICAL PERSONALISM

1. *Biblical Personalism and Man's Ethical Existence*

The confrontations of biblical religion and ontology, in our second chapter, were restricted to the objective side of religion, to the doctrinal contents of biblical faith, and to the conceptual forms of ontological thought. We have not yet touched on the situation of man in the state of faith and, correspondingly, on the situation of man in the state of asking for ultimate reality. It is now necessary to analyze the subjective side of biblical religion and to confront it with the subjective side of the ontological task. This confrontation, however, will bring us to the point where the positive relation between biblical religion and ontology comes to light for the first time. It will be the turning point from the preliminary confrontation to a strong and final one. The latter will be worked out in opposite order, starting with the subjective side of biblical religion and returning in the last chapter to the objective side, until we have reached that with which we have begun, the idea of God in its relation to the ultimate reality for which ontology asks.

Man's existence in relation to God, in view of biblical religion, is, above all, ethical existence. In the first chapters of Genesis this is abundantly expressed and with tremendous emphasis. Man is put into paradise with a commandment and a prohibition. He experiences temptation and decides against the commandment; he loses his innocence and the unity with nature and other men. New temptations arise, and man becomes the killer of his brother. The anxiety of guilt drives him from place to place. Moral depravity spreads and brings the flood over mankind. The covenant between God and the elected nation has as its "Magna Carta" the Mosaic law, including the Decalogue. The prophetic wrath turns against those who use the covenant for injustice, and the whole history of Israel is determined by the problem of obedience and disobedience of leaders and people alike. John the Baptist makes the kinship with Abraham dependent on the fulfilment of the law. Jesus reinterprets the law, shows its radical implications, and sums it up in the commandment of love. All the New Testament books, Paul's epistles as well as that of James, are full of ethical material. The writer of the Johannine literature, in spite of his

44

mystical and ontological tendencies, is especially emphatic about the law of love, the disregard of which destroys the relation to God.

All this is well known; but sometimes we should expose ourselves to the overwhelming weight of ethical material in biblical religion. And, if we do so, we should be aware of the way in which biblical personalism deals with ethics. Man is always put before a decision. He must decide for or against Yahweh, for or against the Christ, for or against the Kingdom of God. Biblical ethics is not a system of virtues and vices, of laws and counsels, of rewards and punishments. All this is not lacking, but it appears within a framework of concrete, personal decisions. Every decision is urgent; it has to be made now. When it has been made, it has far-reaching consequences. It is always an ultimate decision—a decision of infinite weight. It decides man's destiny. It decides the destiny of nations, the selected one as much as the others. Every generation in every nation has to decide for or against righteousness, for or against him who is the God of righteousness. And in every nation, including the selected one, the decision against righteousness means self-destruction. No sacramental activity, even if it is done in God's name, can save the violator of the law of justice from

45

the wrath of God. The ethical decision determines the destiny of the individual: his eternal destiny depends on his decision for or against the Christ. But the decision for or against the Christ is made by people who do not even know his name. What is decisive is only whether they act for or against the law of love, for which the Christ stands. Acting according to it means being received in the unity of fulfilment. Acting against it means being excluded from fulfilment and being cast into the despair of nonbeing. This is biblical ethics. It has little to do with the middle-class ethics of avoiding a few things which are supposed to be wrong and doing a few things which are supposed to be right. Biblical ethics means standing in ultimate decisions for or against God. Biblical ethics makes us persons, because it places us before this decision.

What has the ontological question, even if it were a matter of ultimate concern, to do with the situation of ethical decision in biblical religion? Is not the a-personal character of the ontological principle opposed to the appeal to decide ethically? Is not the cognitive *eros* of the philosopher indifferent to the demands of the God of love? Does not the ultimate principle of ontology disregard the contrast between good and evil? Is not the religious background of ontology mystical participation, whereas biblical religion presupposes the distance of ethical command and ethical obedience? Does not ontology deprive biblical religion of its unconditional ethical passion? Is not Kierkegaard right when he accuses Hegel of sacrificing the ethically deciding person to the aesthetic distance of theoretical intuition?

Does this not mean that the confrontation has reached a point at which a synthesis between ontological thought and biblical religion has proved to be not only impossible but ethically dangerous and objectionable?

2. Biblical Personalism and Man's Social Existence

What has been said about man's ethical existence is confirmed also in man's social existence. God calls families, nations, groups within the nation, the group which transcends all nations, the "assembly of God," the church. And God's purpose in history is to save individuals, not as individuals, but as participants in his kingdom, in the unity of all beings under God. Therefore, the message of the prophets and apostles is given to groups. They are called individually, but their message is destined for the nation to which they belong or for the church of which they are members. They are not strangers in the

47

group to which they give judgment and promise. They live and think and talk within the experiences and traditions of their people. They use their symbols and deal with their problems. This is the reason for the conservative attitude of the Old Testament prophets toward the religion of the past, of Jesus and the apostles toward the Old Testament, and, to anticipate later biblicistic movements, of the Reformers toward the early church. The prophet does not leave the community, though he may be thrown out of it; but he turns one element of the tradition against a distorted tradition in which this element has been forgotten. The prophet does not intend to create a new community, and just for this reason he often does it against his will. The prophet needs solitude, not the loneliness of separation, but the solitude of him who takes the group spiritually with him into his solitude in order to return to it bodily. Biblical religion speaks frequently of the solitude of the "men of God" but seldom of their loneliness and separation from the group which rejects them.

The ontological question is raised in loneliness, even if the lonely thinker participates in the life of the group as an ordinary member. The loneliness of the philosopher was experienced by many of them. It was experienced by Heraclitus, whom it drove into bitterness and arrogance. It was experienced by Socrates, who accepted it and gave an example of the courage which takes such loneliness upon one's self. It was experienced by the Stoics, who in the midst of political activities felt lonely as the bearers of wisdom in a world of fools. It was the experience of Spinoza, whose philosophical loneliness was akin to the loneliness of the mystic. It was the experience of the ancient skeptics who went into the desert never to return. It was the experience of those modern skeptics who hid themselves under many masks from intolerance in periods of dogmatism. It cannot be otherwise, for the first step of the creative philosopher is radical doubt. He questions not only the traditions and symbols of the community to which he belongs but also what is called the "natural world view," the common-sense presuppositions of "everybody." He who seriously asks the question: "Why is there something, why not nothing?" has experienced the shock of nonbeing and has in thought transcended everything given in nature and mankind. He has dissolved (usually without intending to do so) the ties with any community of belief. Again one may ask: Is it not impossible to unite the solitude of the prophet which binds him to the community with the loneliness of the philosopher which separates him from the community? And does not every one of us, whether bound by biblical religion or driven to radical doubt, experience something of the destiny of the prophet and the philosopher within himself, although perhaps in a less extreme form?

It is this conflict which underlies the present discussion about *eros* and *agape*. Biblical religion demands and gives that kind of love which the New Testament calls *agape*. Philosophy, from Plato on, praises the *eros* which carries the soul in its search for ultimate reality. If *agape* and *eros* exclude each other, the case for a synthesis between biblical religion and ontology is hopeless. *Agape* seeks that which is concrete, individual, unique, here and now. *Agape* seeks the person, the other one who cannot be exchanged for anything or anyone else. He cannot be subsumed under abstractions. He must be accepted in spite of the universals which try to prevent his acceptance, such as moral judgments based on general norms, or social differences justifying indifference or hostility, or psychological characteristics inhibiting a full community with him. *Agape* accepts the concrete in spite of the power of the universal which tries to swallow the concrete. *Eros*—a word which is not used by biblical religion—intuits the universals, the eternal essences (ideas), of which the concrete is only a weak imitation. *Eros* drives beyond the individual things and persons. It uses the concrete as a starting point. But then it transcends it and dissolves it into the universal. The fulfilment of *eros* is the mystical union with the one, in which all concreteness has disappeared. Ontological passion has the character of *eros*. The affirmation of the other one in his concreteness is *agape*. Is a union possible between these two? Does not the search for ultimate reality contradict not only hope and faith but also love? And how can something which denies love be united with biblical religion?

3. *Faith and Sin in Biblical Religion*

Man's ethical and social existence in the Bible is based on his religious existence. The biblical word for religious existence is "faith." Only in this sense will it be used here and in the following lecture. Faith is the state of being grasped by an ultimate concern. And, since only that which is the ground of our being and meaning should concern us ultimately, we can also say: Faith is the concern about our existence in its ultimate "whence" and "whither." It is a concern of the whole person; it is the most personal concern and that which determines all others. It is not something that can be forced upon us; it is not something which we can produce by the will to believe, but that by which we are grasped. It is, in biblical terminology, the divine Spirit working in our spirit which creates faith. Such a concept of faith has little to do with the popular concepts of faith as the belief in something unbelievable, as the subjection to an authority in which we trust, or as the risk of accepting something as highly probable but not certain. Such concepts, for which the theologians are as much responsible as popular misunderstanding, lie beneath the level on which the confrontation of ontology and biblical religion must take place. It would be good if philosophers and scientists stopped accusing religion of what is the most frequent distortion of religion—the intellectualistic and voluntaristic misconception of faith. However, if the concept of faith is so frequently and so radically distorted, and if even theologians and, one must add, much ordinary preaching and teaching of the church are responsible for it, is there not an element in the biblical concept of faith which drives almost irresistibly to its misconception? And is not the personalistic character of the biblical concept of faith precisely the cause of this situation? And, finally, is it not just this situation which definitely prevents a synthesis between biblical faith and autonomous reason?

Faith, in the biblical view, is an act of the whole personality. Will, knowledge, and emotion participate in it. It is an act of self-surrender, of obedience, of assent. Each of these elements must be present. Emotional surrender without assent and obedience would by-pass the personal center. It would be a compulsion and not a decision. Intellectual assent without emotional participation distorts religious existence into a nonpersonal, cognitive act. Obedience of the will without assent and emotion leads into a depersonalizing slavery. Faith unites and transcends the special functions of the human mind; it is the most personal act of the person. But each function of the human mind is inclined to a kind of imperialism. It tries to become independent and to control the others. Even biblical religion is not without symptoms of these trends. Faith sometimes approaches the point of emotional ecstasy, sometimes the point of mere moral obedience, sometimes the point of cognitive subjection to an authority.

Biblical faith is the faith of a community, a nation, or a church. He who participates in this faith participates in its symbolic and ritual expressions. The community unavoidably formulates its own foundations in statements which reveal its difference from other groups and protect it against distortions. He who joins the community of faith must accept the statements of faith, the creed of the community. He must assent before he can be received. This assent may be the expression of a genuine personal surrender, but it can become a merely intellectual assent and support the tendency to reduce faith to a cognitive act. At the same time the term "faith" may change its meaning. Instead of designating the state of being grasped by an unconditional concern, it may designate a set of doctrines, as it does in phrases like the "Christian faith," the "faith of the church," the "preservation of our faith," or, in classical terms, *fides quae creditur* ("the faith which is believed"). Biblical religion is not without tendencies in this direction. It could not be otherwise, because it was the religion of a community, the early church.

But, if this is the case, how can there be a synthesis with the radical doubt and the radical search for truth which characterize ontology? Is not the destruction of faith, the withdrawal from the believing assent to anything whatsoever, the condition of an honest philosophizing? And is ontology not developed in the power of human reason, in an attitude of criticism and detachment, which is just the opposite of acceptance and personal surrender? Does not ontology request an attitude of depersonalized objectivity, which contradicts biblical personalism in this as in all other respects? And, if ontology replaces faith, does it not replace the whole biblical religion? One central concept of biblical religion, sin, has been only briefly mentioned. It is a religious concept designating the opposite of faith. The essence of sin is disbelief, the state of estrangement from God, the flight from him, the rebellion against him, the elevation of preliminary concerns to the rank of ultimate concern. Man is bound to sin in all parts of his being, because he is estranged from God in his personal center. Neither his emotion, his will, nor his intellect is excepted from sin and, consequently, from the perversion of their true nature. His intellectual power is as distorted and weakened as his moral power. Neither of them is able to produce reunion with God. According to biblical religion, intellectual endeavor can as little attain the ultimate truth as moral endeavor can attain the ultimate good. He who attempts it deepens the estrangement. This was the message of Paul, Augustine, and Luther. Only he who in the state of faith participates in the good and the true can act according to the norms of truth. Participation precedes action and thought, for participation gives a new being in which sin, or estrangement, is conquered. And participation in that which is of ultimate concern is faith. This means

that the faith which conquers sin, by receiving rec-
onciliation and a new being, must precede the search
for ultimate reality, for the truth itself. Only in the
new state of things can being itself be reached.

Ontology uses man's rational power. It does not
ask the question of sin and salvation. It does not distinguish between original and distorted reason, nor
does it envisage a renewed reason. It starts where it
is and goes ahead toward being-itself. The Bible
often criticizes philosophy, not because it uses reason, but because it uses unregenerated reason for the
knowledge of God. But only the Spirit of God
knows God and gives knowledge of God to those
who are grasped by him, who are in the state of
faith. As in the beginning, so we must ask at the end
of this confrontation: Is there any way to unite the
opposite ways of ontology and biblical religion?
The answer seems to be that the conflict is insoluble.
Point after point (first in the objective and then in
the subjective side of biblical religion) showed a
seeming incompatibility with the ontological attempt. Many people never go beyond this confrontation and draw the consequences in the one or the
other direction. It is understandable that some reject
biblical religion completely because they are called
in the depth of their being, in their intellectual and

moral conscience, to ask the radical question—the question of being and nonbeing. They become heretics or pagans rather than bow to a religion which prohibits the ontological question. It is equally understandable that many faithful Christians shy away from the dangers of the ontological question which makes doubtful that which is most sacred and of infinite significance for them. Neither of these ways is acceptable to some of us, and I believe that neither of them is a service to truth and consequently to God. But, if we try a third way, we must be prepared for the reaction of people who doubt that a third way is possible.

Since the breakdown of the great synthesis between Christianity and the modern mind as attempted by Schleiermacher, Hegel, and nineteenth-century liberalism, an attitude of weariness has grasped the minds of people who are unable to accept one or the other alternative. They are too disappointed to try another synthesis after so many have failed. But there is no choice for us. We must try again! And we want to try by asking the question: Do the attitudes and concepts of biblical religion have implications which not only allow but demand a synthesis with the search for ultimate reality? And, conversely, does not ontological thought have implications which open it for the concern of biblical religion?

4. *Faith, Doubt, and the Ontological Question*

With these questions in mind, we turn to an analysis of the relation of faith and doubt. Here the first, and in some sense all-determining decision must be sought.

A preparation for this decision has already been given in the first chapter in the discussion of the two elements in the attitude of the philosopher, the theoretical and the existential. We spoke of a union of rationality and passion, of detachment and involvement. There is man standing between being and nonbeing, realizing both his finitude and the infinite to which he belongs, asking the question of being. He is infinitely concerned about being, since his very existence is involved in this question. Faith also, as we have seen, is a matter of infinite interest; it is the state of being grasped by the ultimate concern. The man who asks the question of ultimate reality and the man who is in the state of faith are equal with respect to the unconditional character of their concern.

But we must go a step further. Two ultimate concerns cannot exist alongside each other. If they did,

58

the one or the other or both would not really be ultimate. Actually, the one comprises the other. The
ultimate concern of the believer is concern about
that which is really ultimate and therefore the
ground of his being and meaning. He implicitly asks
the question of ultimate reality; he must assume, as
every Christian believer must, that in the symbols of
his ultimate concern the answer to the question of
ultimate reality is implied. As a believer, he is not
concerned with ontological research; but he is concerned with truth, and this means with ultimate reality. Only if God is ultimate reality, can he be our
unconditional concern; only then can he be the object of surrender, obedience, and assent. Faith in anything which has only preliminary reality is idola-
trous. It gives ultimacy to a preliminary concern.
Faith includes the ontological question, whether the
question is asked explicitly or not. The church, from
earliest times, was aware of this fact and made the
question explicit in the moment in which it met the
ontological concern in the Hellenistic world. This is
the reason why we should not accept the type of
biblicism which has been expounded by Ritschl and
Harnack. They accused the early church of having
betrayed biblical religion by relating it positively to
the search for ultimate reality. What Harnack has

called the Hellenization of the gospel was actually the acceptance of the ontological question on the basis of biblical religion. This was inescapable not only because of the necessity of introducing the gospel into the Hellenistic world but also because the discovery of the ontological question by the Greek mind is universally relevant. It is an expression of the human situation as such. On this point, the early church was right, however questionable its concrete solutions may have been, and its nineteenth-century critics were wrong, however great our gratitude for their courageous and successful analysis of the traditional dogma may be.

Faith comprises the ontological question. But is not ontology like a strange body within the body of faith, and, if it is made explicit, does it not destroy faith with its most powerful weapon, namely, doubt? Should not faith keep ontology within its womb, never giving birth to it? Or, in a nonmetaphorical expression, must not the church keep the search for ultimate reality within the limits of its authority—as the Roman church actually does?

This is the fundamental question of the relation of faith and doubt. Faith and doubt do not essentially contradict each other. Faith is the continuous tension between itself and the doubt within itself. This tension does not always reach the strength of a struggle; but, latently, it is always present. This distinguishes faith from logical evidence, scientific probability, traditionalistic self-certainty, and unquestioning authoritarianism. Faith includes both an immediate awareness of something unconditional and the courage to take the risk of uncertainty upon itself. Faith says "Yes" in spite of the anxiety of "No." It does not remove the "No" of doubt and the anxiety of doubt; it does not build a castle of doubt-free security —only a neurotically distorted faith does that—but it takes the "No" of doubt and the anxiety of insecurity into itself. Faith embraces itself and the doubt about itself. Therefore it comprises itself and the ontological question, whose precondition is the radical doubt. Such a faith does not need to be afraid of the free search for ultimate reality. It does not need to keep ontology in ecclesiastical seclusion. It is Protestant by nature, whether it appears in Protestant or in biblical religion.

The philosopher is in a situation which also unites a "No" and "Yes." As we maintained in the first chapter, asking presupposes both a having and a not-having. One cannot ask the ontological question without having at least a prephilosophical knowledge of what "being" means. Everyone participates

61

in being, and everyone experiences being when he encounters beings: persons, things, events, essences. And everyone participates in nonbeing and experiences it in disintegration and in death, in guilt and in doubt. It is this concrete situation in which the philosopher searches for ultimate reality. Like the believer, he lives in a definite world of experiences and symbols. He is not bound to them, but neither is he separated from them. He doubts what he knows, but he does so on the basis of something else he knows; for there is no "No" without a preceding "Yes." *The philosopher has not and has; the believer has and has not.* This is the basis on which ontology and biblical religion find each other. The last chapter will relate the various points of confrontation from this perspective.

VII

THE ONTOLOGICAL PROBLEMS IMPLIED IN THE SUBJECTIVE SIDE OF BIBLICAL RELIGION

1. *Total and Intellectual Conversion*

The third chapter led us to the turning point of this whole book: the problem of faith and doubt in biblical religion and ontology. It disclosed a structural identity of the two, whereas in the preceding chapters only the conflict was shown in its radical and shocking character. In the discussion of faith and doubt, definite analogies of structure between the conflicting sides became visible for the first time. In both biblical religion and ontology an ultimate concern is the driving force; in both of them the "No" of doubt is taken into the "Yes" of courage; in both of them a participation in concrete experiences and symbols gives content to question and answer; in both cases an ultimate trust in the power of being makes human surrender and search possible. This analogy of structure keeps one side open for the other. Both stand on the boundary line between

"Yes" and "No," between being and nonbeing. The ultimate concern about truth which drives toward the search for ultimate reality is a part of the ultimate concern about one's existence as a person, as a being who is able to ask the question of his being and of universal being.

On the basis of this analysis of faith and doubt in biblical religion and ontology, we will now re-examine what seemed to be irreconcilable conflicts in our first confrontation. We will go backward from a confrontation of the biblical view of the human situation to confrontations of the main characteristics of biblical personalism with ontology.

Reason, according to the theological view, not only is finite and therefore unable to grasp the infinite but is also estranged from its essential goodness. Reason stands, like everything in man, under the bondage of estrangement. There is no part of man that is excepted from the universal destiny of sin. For the cognitive function of man's spiritual life this means that reason is blinded and has become unable to recognize God. The eyes of reason must be opened by the revelatory presence of the divine Spirit in the human spirit. Only when this happens can truth be received by human reason.

There is a surprising analogy to this idea in the history of philosophy. Some of the greatest of those who have searched for ultimate reality spoke in a way that is very similar to the way in which the Bible speaks. The term "blindness" for the ordinary state of mind is used in all periods of philosophical thought. The experience of being awakened out of the sleep of the natural world view, the sudden awareness of the light of the ontological question, the breaking-through the surface on which one lived and moved before—these events are described like a religious conversion. Those who are awakened to the light ask passionately the question of ultimate reality. They are different from those who do not. As Plato described it, they are no longer bound to the shadows of the cave; they are liberated and able to see true reality. They have experienced a saving transformation and an illuminating revelation. Only because this has happened to them can they seriously and successfully ask the question of ultimate reality. Ontology presupposes a conversion, an opening of the eyes, a revelatory experience. It is not a matter of detached observation, analysis, and hypothesis. Only he who is involved in ultimate reality, only he who has encountered it as a matter of existential concern, can try to speak about it meaningfully. In this sense one must say that there is faith in the philosopher, not a faith that believes in given doctrines (this is not faith but belief), but faith as the state of being grasped by ultimate reality. If the term "philosophical faith" can be used at all, it should be used in the sense of "faith in ultimate reality," the genuine object of the love of wisdom.

Certainly philosophical conversion and philosophical faith are not identical with conversion and faith in biblical religion. The latter are related equally to all functions of man's spiritual life, to his whole personality. There is no preponderance of the cognitive function as it is in philosophical conversion and philosophical faith. But even philosophical conversion and philosophical faith are not restricted to the cognitive function, for this function, if it is existentially moved, cannot be separated from the other functions. Philosophical conversion changes not only the thinking of the philosopher but also his being. But his being remains in the background, while in religious conversion it is in the foreground. Religious conversion, therefore, is more embracing. It includes the possibility of philosophical conversion, just as religious faith includes the possibility of ontological awareness. Not in everyone—actually only in a few—does this possibility become actuality. But in everyone it is a possibility.

2. *Ethics of Grace and Ethics of Decision*

When we first confronted ontology with the ethical character of biblical religion, there were two sides of man's ethical existence in which the conflict seemed to be insoluble: the situation of decision and the distance between God and man. The Bible is aware of the intrinsic problems of them both. We decide, we believe that we are able to decide, and after the decision we realize that it was not our own power but a power which decided through us. If we make a decision for what we essentially are, and therefore ought to be, it is a decision out of grace. If it is a decision contrary to what we essentially are, it is a decision in a state of being possessed or inhabited by demonic spirits. As Luther expressed it, man is like a horse, ridden either by God or by the devil. But neither the Bible nor the Reformers believe that this situation takes away man's responsibility and his freedom of decision. It includes, however, a profound ontological problem—that of freedom and destiny. A theologian who explains the way in which Paul combines his emphasis on God working everything in the process of our salvation with his appeal to us to work out our own salvation uses the categories "freedom" and "destiny," although he does not employ these words. But he who uses these categories even implicitly must know their genuine meaning; he must describe the ontological structure to which they belong. In the third chapter it seemed that freedom is an ethical concept, while destiny is an ontological one. But now the religious concept of grace has shown that this is not so—that the concepts both of freedom and of destiny belong to ontology as well as to ethics and that both are transcended and united in the religious symbol of sin and grace. This refers not only to individuals, but, in a more limited way, to groups also and, finally, to the whole of world history.

The other main point of conflict between ontology and the ethical character of biblical religion is that between participation and obedience. Ontological awareness of the ground of being presupposes participation. The ethical situation demands obedience involving the separation between him who commands and him who obeys. In biblical religion this problem is recognized and dealt with in terms of the "law of love." This term contains in itself the tension between participation and distance. It is a law; and the law stands above me and possibly against me. But it is the law of love, and love is the power that unites that which is separated. Biblical, classical, and mystical Christianity agree in the assertion that the moral act, in order to be perfect or even possible, must follow from the union of God and man in the love toward God, which is the answer to God's love toward man. He who is united with the will of God voluntarily acts and does more than any law commands. He acts out of participation, not out of the relation of command and obedience. He who does not participate in the being of God, which is the being of love, cannot act according to God's being. He who does not participate in the good itself cannot be good. Again, Paul makes this participation dependent upon the divine Spirit, and the divine Spirit is nothing other than God dynamically present in us. Without this participation neither the knowledge of God nor the love of God is possible. The union of participation does not fall upon the ontological side and the distance of obedience on the ethical side. Both sides are ontological and ethical, and both are united and transcended in the concept of love. Therefore, we need not only an ethics of love but, following Augustine, also an ontology of love. Whoever attempts to explain the relationship of love and law employs the basic ontological categories of participation and individualization, and he presupposes the ontological conflict between essential and existential being (without which there would be no law which stands against us). As a theologian, one should not be unaware of the categories one uses even if one tries to avoid philosophical terms.

3. *Solitude and Love in Biblical Religion and Ontology*

We have confronted the loneliness of the philosopher with the social relatedness of the prophet and the *eros* which drives toward the search for ultimate reality with the *agape* of biblical religion. But this is not the last word about the problem. First of all, the prophet and every religious man knows not only the solitude of withdrawal but also the loneliness of the ultimate situation. There are moments (descriptions of which fill the pages of religious literature) in which the religious man feels deserted by man, by God, and by himself. The traditions and symbols of the community to which he belongs have become meaningless to him. He realizes the finitude, the limits of participation, the unreality of his world. He experiences the loneliness of his having to die and of his personal guilt. On the other hand, the philosopher does not remain in loneliness. He returns to the group from which he has intentionally separated himself through his radical asking. All classical philosophers have tried to mediate their insights to the group from which they came. They criticized myths and morals, conventions and prejudices, often as passionately as did the prophets. The search for ultimate reality did not make them insensitive to the predicament of those with whom they lived. Often they reacted to the situation of their contemporaries with prophetic wrath, prophetic despair, and prophetic hope. And some of them became martyrs like the prophets. He who speaks out of the situation of faith and he who speaks out of the search for ultimate reality both have the experience that the people to whom they speak have ears and do not hear and eyes and do not see. Ontology, as much as biblical religion, is a stumbling block for the people who go along the ordinary way of theoretical and practical conventions. And both the ontological and the religious messages bring burdens and dangers to those who have to pronounce them.

The relation of ontology and biblical religion to man's social existence is being discussed implicitly under the heading: "*eros* and *agape*." Where *agape* (the biblical term for "love") is put into an absolute contrast to *eros* (the Platonic term for "love"), no positive relation of biblical religion to ontology is seen. But this presupposes a distortion of the meaning both of *agape* and of *eros*. The New Testament does not use the term *eros*, because *eros* had received at that time an anti-Platonic, exclusively sensual meaning. But the New Testament teaches explicitly and implicitly that participation in the divine Spirit or Logos means both having love and having truth. The desire for God is both the desire for him as love and the desire for him as truth. If the desire for him as love is called *agape*, the desire for him as truth should be called *eros*. And this would correspond with the genuine meaning of *eros* (e.g., in Plato's *Symposium*). *Eros* drives the soul through all levels of reality to ultimate reality, to truth itself, which is the good itself. In later antiquity the unity of love and the quest for ultimate reality are expressed in the threefold meaning of the word "gnosis" as knowledge, sexual intercourse, and mystical union. Certainly *agape* adds a decisive element to the ancient idea of love, but it does not deny the drive for cognitive union with ultimate reality. *Agape* reaches down to the lowest, forgiving its estrangement and reuniting it with the highest. But *agape* does not contradict the desire for the highest; and a part of this desire is cognitive *eros*.

VIII

THE ONTOLOGICAL PROBLEMS IMPLIED IN THE OBJECTIVE SIDE OF BIBLICAL RELIGION

1. *The Divine Manifestations and the Search for Ultimate Reality*

We have confronted three symbols of the divine self-manifestation (creation, the Christ, the *eschaton*) with some ontological concepts and have found seemingly insuperable contradictions between them. Again I want to show that such contradictions are not necessary and that each of these symbols demands and has received ontological interpretation.

Creation by the Word out of nothing describes the absolute independence of God as creator, the absolute dependence of creation, and the infinite gap between them. The ontological question arises immediately at several points. One must ask how the eternal Logos, the principle of God's self-manifestation, is related to the contents of the world process. The classical answer, that the essences or potentialities of the world are eternal in the divine "mind," must either be accepted or be replaced by another one—and every answer is necessarily ontological.

Theology has rightly insisted that the "nothing" out of which the world is created is not the *me on* of the Greeks, that is, the matter which receives and resists the creative act. But, if the answer of a dualistic ontology is rejected, one must seek for another answer to the question: What does this "nothing" mean? How is it related to the divine, which as life presupposes nonbeing? Can one perhaps say in a highly symbolic phrase that the divine life is the eternal conquest of the nonbeing which belongs to him? Whatever the answer may be, it is ontological.

If we ask about the relation of the divine creation to the divine preservation and answer with Augustine that preservation is the permanent creativity of God in everything that is, we have reached the ontological metaphor "ground of being." And if we ask about the meaning of the ever repeated assertion that God is both *in* and *above* the world and question the use of the spatial metaphors "in" and "above," we have asked an ontological question. If we then answer that the relation of God and the world is not spatial but must be expressed in terms of creative freedom, an ontological answer is given, but an answer in terms of freedom. The freedom of the creature to act against its essential unity with God makes God transcendent to the world.

Such ontology of freedom does not deprive existence of its sinful character, as an ontology of necessity would do. But, at the same time, it states the universality of the fall in terms of the concept of destiny which stands in an ontological polarity with the concept of freedom.

The christological confrontation has led to the question: Is there a necessary conflict between the universal Logos and the Logos who is present in the personal life of Jesus as the Christ? The early church and, following it, the church in most periods did not believe in such an unavoidable conflict. The Logos (i.e., the divine self-manifestation) is actively present in everything that exists, because everything is made through it. But only the ultimate divine self-manifestation shows what Luther has called the heart of divinity, God for man, eternal God-manhood in its very center. The Logos universal and the Logos as the power of a personal life are one and the same Logos. Only against the background of the universal Logos is the incarnate Logos a meaningful concept. Biblical religion has shown the ontological implications of one of its fundamental assertions in the prologue of the Fourth Gospel. Ontology is able to receive the christological question—the question of the place in which the universal Logos manifests itself existentially and unconditionally; the universal Logos appears in a concrete form. Every philosophy shows the traits of its birthplace. Every philosophy has concrete existential roots. To say that Jesus as the Christ is the concrete place where the Logos becomes visible is an assertion of faith and can be made only by him who is grasped by the Christ as the manifestation of his ultimate concern. But it is not an assertion which contradicts or is strange to the search for ultimate reality. The name "Jesus the Christ" implies an ontology.

The third manifestation of God which we have confronted with ontological categories is history, running toward an end, the historical-eschatological element in biblical religion.

Here again the first answer to the question is that only special kinds of ontology make the historically new impossible, for example, circular interpretation of the temporal processes. If time is symbolized as a circle, the new is excluded; everything repeats itself. The same is true of mechanical determinism in which a given state of things has necessary consequences, calculable in principle for all following states. But such ontologies do not represent ontology as such. The philosophies of life and process which have roots in men like Augustine and Duns Scotus have emphasized the openness of reality toward the future and have made a place for the contingent, the new, the unique, the irrepeatable. And no theologian who interprets the Bible through Greek terms like "history" can escape the profoundly ontological question: how history is related to nature; how all history is related to the small section of world historical events with which biblical religion deals; how the events in which man is involved are related to the events in the whole universe.

And there is another, even more difficult, question which demands an ontological answer implied in the historical-eschatological view of biblical religion. It is the meaning of the *eschaton* or the relation of the temporal and the eternal. If one identifies the eternal with the temporal continuation of life after death, one has made an ontological statement, and a very poor one, by confusing eternity with endless temporality. If one, in opposition to this, says that eternity is the simple negation of temporality, one has also made an ontological statement, also a very bad one, by confusing eternity with timelessness. There is, however, a third answer, also ontological, which does justice to the meaning both of time and of eternity. Eternity transcends and contains temporality, but a temporality which is not subject to the law of finite transitoriness, a temporality in which past and future are united, though not negated in the eternal presence. History then runs toward its end in the eternal, and the eternal participates in the moments of time, judging and elevating them to the eternal. Such statements are ontological in a half-symbolic gown. No theologian can escape them. And those who use a primitive-mythological language deceive themselves if they do not realize that the phrase "life after death" contains an ontology of a highly questionable character.

2. The Divine-Human Relationship and the Search for Ultimate Reality

God speaks to man in biblical religion. The *word*, literally taken, is a spoken sound or a written sign, pointing to a meaning with which it is conventionally connected. But it is obvious that the God of the Bible does not speak or hear in this way. His Word is an event created by the divine Spirit in the human spirit. It is both driving power and infinite meaning. The Word of God is God's creative self-manifestation and not a conversation between two beings. Therefore, the Word is one of the aspects of God himself; it is God manifesting himself to himself. It is an expression of God as living and, as trinitarian thinking has always realized, an element in the power of being itself. It is ontological in its implications, although it is a genuinely religious symbol. This makes the doctrines of creation and salvation through the Logos possible and necessary, and it should make it impossible to confuse a theology of the Word with a theology of talk. The Word is an element in ultimate reality; it is the power of being, expressing itself in many forms, in nature and history, in symbols and sacraments, in silent and in spoken words. But it is not bound to spoken words. The nature of the word is a problem as old as ontology, and the divine Word is a symbol as old as religion. Without knowing something about the nature of the word, without an ontology of the Logos, theology cannot interpret the speaking of God, the divine Word. But, if theology uses this insight into the ontological nature of the word, it can teach meaningfully about the nature of the divine Word, the Logos who is with God.

The most devastating conflict between biblical religion and ontology appears to be the conflict between reciprocity and participation in the divine-human relationship. Ontology seems to remove the living interdependence between God and man, and it seems to remove the meaning of prayer, especially of the prayer of supplication.

The problem is present within biblical religion itself in the tensions between the unconditional emphasis on God's working in everything, even evil, sin, and death, and human responsibility for good and evil. A divine determinism often seems to conquer biblical personalism, and in men like Augustine, Thomas, Luther, and Calvin this determinism reaches sharpest expression. But at no point do these men and the biblical writers allow their emphasis on the divine activity to destroy the divine-human reciprocity. This can be understood only through the ontological polarity of freedom and destiny and through a distinction between the levels of being, namely, between the ground of being, which transcends all polarities, and finite being, which is subjected to them.

The divine determinism of biblical thought does not make the prayer of supplication impossible. No religious act expresses more obviously the reciprocity between God and man. Without the presupposition that the prayer changes the will of God in some respect, whether he hears or rejects the prayer, no prayer of supplication seems to be meaningful. But the early theologians, whose prayers underlie most of the Christian liturgies, emphasized the unchangeability of God against all paganism. God, the immovable, the transcendent One, was the first object of their theology. They were thoroughly ontological, and their relation to God was thoroughly reciprocal and full of prayer, including the prayer of supplication. This was and is possible because every serious prayer includes surrender to the will of God. It is aware of the ultimate inadequacy of words, the literal meaning of which is the attempt to move the divine will into the direction of one's own will. In every true prayer God is both he to whom we pray and he who prays through us. For it is the divine Spirit who creates the right prayer. At this point the ontological structure which makes God an object of us as subjects is infinitely transcended. God stands in the divine-human reciprocity, but only as he who transcends it and comprises both sides of the reciprocity. He reacts, but he reacts to that which is his own act working through our finite freedom. He never can become a mere object. This is the limit of the symbols of reciprocity. This makes the ontological question necessary.

3. God as the Ground of Being in Ontology and Biblical Religion

Our confrontation of biblical religion and the search for ultimate reality started with the doctrine of God. And our attempts to show the ultimate unity of ontology and biblical personalism must return to the doctrine of God. It is the beginning and the end of all theological thought. There is an element in the biblical and ecclesiastical idea of God which makes the ontological question necessary. It is the assertion that God *is.* Of course not everyone asks what this word "is" in relation to God means. Most people, including the biblical writers, take the word in its popular sense: something "is" if it can be found in the whole of potential experience. That which can be encountered within the whole of reality is real. Even the more sophisticated discussions about the existence or nonexistence of God often have this popular tinge. But, if God can be found within the whole of reality, then the whole of reality is the basic and dominant concept. God, then, is subject to the structure of reality. As in Greek religion, fate was above Zeus, determining him and his decisions, so God would be subject to the polarities and categories of reality as constituting his fate. The fight against this dangerous consequence of biblical personalism started in the Bible itself and continued in all periods of church history. The God who is *a* being is transcended by the God who is Being itself, the ground and abyss of every being. And the God who is *a* person is transcended by the God who is the Personal-Itself, the ground and abyss of every person. In statements like these, religion and ontology meet. Without philosophies in which the ontological question we have raised appears, Christian theology would have been unable to interpret the nature of the being of God to those who wanted to know in what sense one can say that God *is*. And the question is asked in prephilosophical, as well as in philosophical, terms by very primitive and very sophisticated people.

This means that *being* and *person* are not contradictory concepts. Being includes personal being; it does not deny it. The ground of being is the ground of personal being, not its negation. The ontological question of being creates not a conflict but a necessary basis for any theoretical dealing with the biblical concept of the personal God. If one starts to think about the meaning of biblical symbols, one is already in the midst of ontological problems.

Religiously speaking, this means that our encounter with the God who is a person includes the encounter with the God who is the ground of everything personal and as such not *a* person. Religious experience, particularly as expressed in the great religions, exhibits a deep feeling for the tension between the personal and the nonpersonal element in the encounter between God and man. The Old as well as the New Testament has the astonishing power to speak of the presence of the divine in such a way that the I-thou character of the relation never darkens the transpersonal power and mystery of the divine, and vice versa. Examples of this can be found in the seemingly simple words of Jesus about the hairs on our head, all of which are counted, and the birds which do not fall without the will of God. These words imply that no single event among the infinite number of events that happen in every infinitely small moment of time happens without the participation of God. If anything transcends primitive personalism, it is such a saying. And it is only a continuation of this line of biblical religion when Luther, who was very suspicious of philosophy, speaks of God as being nearer to all creatures than they are to themselves, or of God being totally present in a grain of sand and at the same time not being comprehended by the totality of all things, or of God giving the power to the arm of the murderer to drive home the murderous knife. Here Luther's sometimes unreflective biblical personalism is transcended, and God as the power of Being in everything is ontologically affirmed.

The correlation of ontology and biblical religion is an infinite task. There is no special ontology which we have to accept in the name of the biblical message, neither that of Plato nor that of Aristotle, neither that of Cusanus nor that of Spinoza, neither that of Kant nor that of Hegel, neither that of Lao-tze nor that of Whitehead. There is no saving ontology, but the ontological question is implied in the question of salvation. To ask the ontological question is a necessary task. *Against* Pascal I say: The God of Abraham, Isaac, and Jacob and the God of the philosophers is the same God. He is a person and the negation of himself as a person.

Faith comprises both itself and the doubt of itself. The Christ is Jesus and the negation of Jesus. Biblical religion is the negation and the affirmation of ontology. To live serenely and courageously in these tensions and to discover finally their ultimate unity in the depths of our own souls and in the depth of the divine life is the task and the dignity of human thought.